VISUALIZATION ADVANTAGE

Winning Architecture Through Client-Focused Design

Architect Mahindra Chawla

VISUALIZATION ADVANTAGE

Winning Architecture Through Client-Focused Design

ISBN: 978-93-343-7383-7
Paperback

First Edition: June 2025

Published by: Chawla N Associates, Mumbai, India
Contact Information:
email VisualizationAdvantage@gmail.com
Website: https://ChawlaNassociates.com

Library of Congress Subject Headings:

- Interior Design Practice
- Architecture – Practice
- Interior Design & Build
- Business Development
- Architectural Drawing Technique
- Client Relations
- Visualization

Printed and Published in India by Mahindra Chawla

Version 1.0 - June 2025

TABLE OF CONTENTS

Introduction

Visualization That Wins Projects

In the competitive world of architecture and design, extraordinary visualization isn't just about creating beautiful images—it's about developing a powerful communication tool that converts prospects into clients and concepts into commissions.

My Journey in Architectural Visualization

When I graduated from L S Raheja School of Architecture in Mumbai in the late 1980s, architectural visualization meant hand-drawn perspectives and physical models. As I moved through my career—from my early days at Space Consultants learning interior fundamentals under Mrs. Kiran Patki, to supervising multi-storied residential buildings in Bandra, to founding an independent practice with my wife Anjali in 1991—I witnessed and participated in the evolution of visualization from artistic skill to strategic business tool.

Over three decades of practice across Mumbai, Bangalore, Delhi, and beyond, our projects have spanned high-end residential interiors, corporate offices, structural repairs, and industrial facilities. Throughout this diverse portfolio, one constant has emerged: the projects we win are not necessarily those with the most technically impressive visualizations, but those with the most strategic visualization—images that speak directly to client needs, concerns, and aspirations.

The Visualization Paradox

This reveals what I call the Visualization Paradox: as visualization technology becomes more sophisticated, the technical quality of images becomes less decisive in winning projects. When everyone can produce photorealistic renderings, the competitive advantage shifts from technical execution to strategic application.

Today's clients aren't evaluating visualization quality on rendering resolution or lighting accuracy—they're responding to how effectively the visualization addresses their specific concerns, communicates project value, and builds confidence in both the design and the design team.

Beyond Beautiful Pictures

This book isn't about creating more beautiful architectural visualization—there are countless technical guides for that. Instead, it focuses on creating more effective visualization: images that connect with clients, build trust, communicate value, and ultimately win projects.

Drawing from hundreds of projects across three decades of practice, I'll share the approaches that have proven most effective in converting visualization from pretty pictures to powerful persuasion. You'll learn:

- *How clients actually "read" architectural visualizations (it's not how architects think they do)*
- *Strategic visualization sequencing that guides clients from interest to commitment*
- *Specialized approaches for different project types, from residential to renovation*

- *Methods for developing a distinctive visualization signature that builds recognition*
- *Practical technology integration that enhances client understanding*
- *How to leverage visualization as a business development tool*

The Core Premise

The central thesis of this book is straightforward: The most successful architectural visualization isn't determined by technical excellence but by strategic application. Understanding when to use which visualization approach with which client type at which decision stage is more valuable than mastering the latest rendering software.

For Practicing Architects and Designers

This book is written specifically for practicing architects and designers who want to win more projects and build stronger practices. It assumes you already know how to create competent visualization—what you're seeking is the strategic understanding to make that visualization more effective in securing work.

Whether you're a sole practitioner looking to grow, a small firm competing against larger offices, or an established practice seeking to enter new markets, the visualization strategies in this book will help you communicate more effectively with clients and convert more prospects into projects

A Note on Examples and Illustrations

Throughout this book, I draw on examples from my own practice across Mumbai and beyond. These examples aren't chosen for their visual impressiveness but for their strategic effectiveness—visualizations that successfully communicated complex ideas, addressed client concerns, and ultimately won projects.

The principles behind these examples are universally applicable, regardless of your geographical location, project types, or visualization technology. Whether you're creating hand sketches or virtual reality experiences, the strategic fundamentals remain consistent.

How to Use This Book

You can read this book from beginning to end for a comprehensive understanding of strategic visualization, or focus on specific chapters addressing your current challenges:

- ***If you're struggling with client communication**, start with Chapter 1 on visualization language*
- ***If you're not converting** initial interest to signed contracts, focus on Chapter 2 on decision sequences*
- ***If you specialize in specific project types**, explore the relevant specialized chapters*
- ***If you're seeking to differentiate your practice**, concentrate on Chapter 6 on the visualization signature*
- ***If you're evaluating technology investments**, prioritize Chapter 7 on practical integration*
- ***If you're focused on business growth**, begin with Chapter 8 on visualization as marketing*

*However you approach it, the goal remains the same: to **transform your visualization from a project delivery component to a powerful tool for practice success.***

Let's begin.

Chapter 1

The Hidden Language of Visualization

What Clients Actually See

When architects and designers present visualization materials, we often assume clients are seeing what we see. This fundamental misunderstanding creates a significant gap between presentation and persuasion.

In my practice spanning hundreds of high-end residential and corporate projects across Mumbai, I've observed a consistent pattern: clients don't "read" architectural visualizations the way professionals do. Where we see spatial relationships, structural solutions, and design language, they see something entirely different.

The Client's Hierarchy of Visual Perception:

1. **Emotional Response** - The immediate feeling the visualization evokes
2. **Lifestyle Compatibility** - How they imagine themselves in the space
3. **Status Signalling** - What the design communicates about their position
4. **Practical Concerns** - How the space will function for their specific needs
5. **Aesthetic Details** - The design elements we often prioritize

This reversed hierarchy explains why technically brilliant visualizations often fail to win projects, while seemingly simpler presentations secure client commitment.

HOW CLIENTS PRIORITIZE VISUAL ELEMENTS

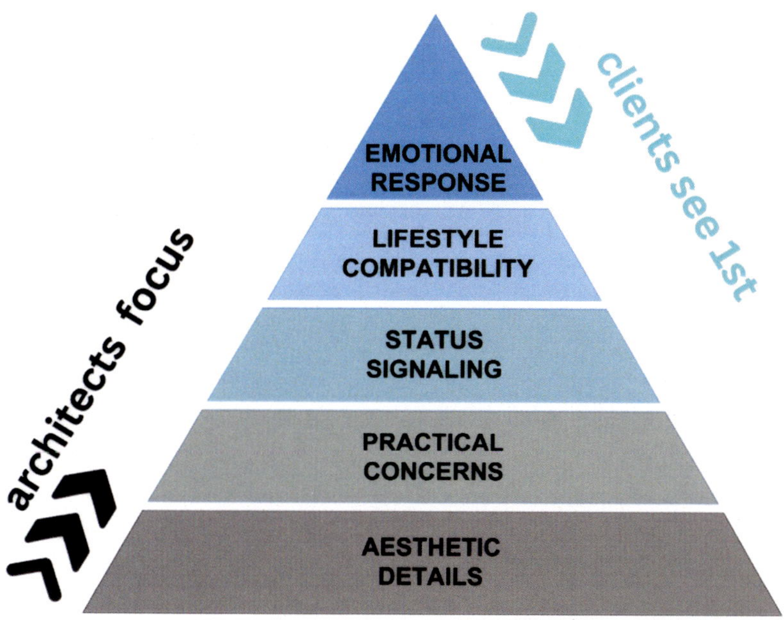

WHERE ARCHITECTS FOCUS STARTS

V/S

WHAT CLIENTS SEE FIRST

THE INVERTED PERCEPTION HIERARCHY

The Emotion-First Approach

Case Study: The Powai Residence Project

When approaching the fourth project for the City Engineer of Thane—a luxury apartment in Powai—I faced competition from three other design firms with impressive technical presentations. Rather than leading with detailed floor plans and technical renderings, we took a different approach.

Our initial presentation contained just five visualizations:

1. A view from the entry showing natural light falling on a family photograph
2. The living area depicted during evening entertainment
3. A morning scene in the kitchen showing breakfast preparation
4. The master bedroom at sunset with Mumbai's skyline visible
5. A detailed view of the custom study with integrated technology

These visualizations contained all the necessary architectural information, but were packaged to trigger an emotional connection first. Technical details were embedded rather than highlighted.

The result? Despite charging a premium above competitors, we secured the project within the first meeting. The client later confided: "Your designs showed us actually living there, not just how the apartment would look."

Breaking the Technical Barrier
Architects are trained to communicate in a specialized visual language that most clients haven't learned to read. Effective visualization requires translating between these languages.

Consider these visualization elements from least to most accessible to clients:

- **Floor Plans** - Often abstract and difficult for clients to interpret spatially
- **Sections** - Even more challenging for non-architects to understand
- **Technical Elevations** - Provide information, but limited emotional connection
- **Perspective Renderings** - Begin to bridge the comprehension gap
- **Experiential Visualizations** - Show the design as it will be experienced
- **Context Visualizations** - Place the design in the client's life context

The paradox: as architects advance in their training, they often move further from the visual language that most effectively communicates with clients.

The Three Layers of Effective Visualization

Every successful project visualization must operate on three levels simultaneously:

1. **The Experience Layer** - How the space feels and functions for users
2. **The Value Layer** - How the design justifies its investment
3. **The Technical Layer** - How the design will be executed

Most architects focus almost exclusively on the technical layer, touch lightly on the experience layer, and neglect the value layer entirely. Yet for clients, this priority is exactly reversed.

EVERY EFFECTIVE VISUALIZATION MUST COMMUNICATE ALL 3 LAYERS SIMULTANEOUSLY

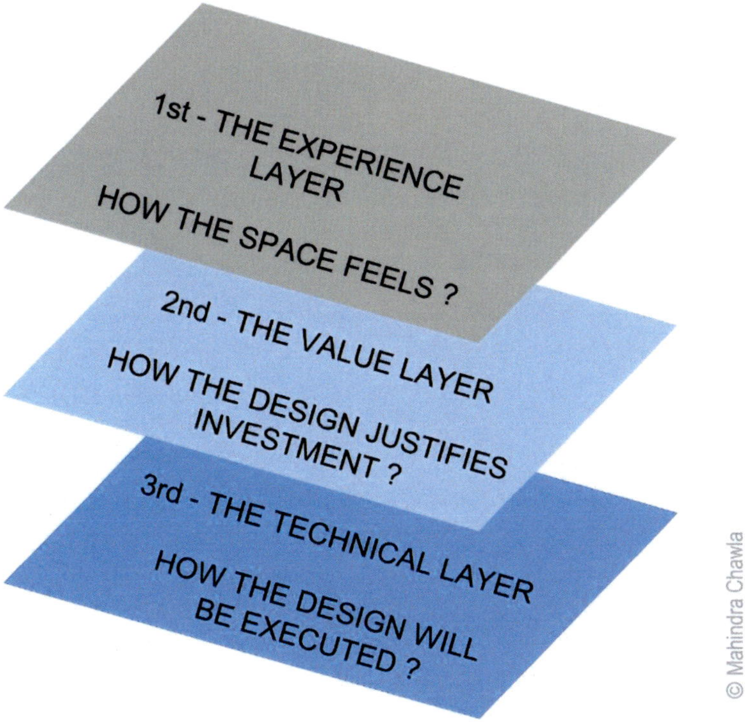

THE 3 LAYERS OF EFFECTIVE VISUALIZATION

Practical Application: The Translation Technique

Before finalizing any visualization for client presentation, run it through this three-question filter:

1. **The Emotional Question**: "What feeling does this visualization evoke in the first three seconds?"
2. **The Value Question**: "Does this visualization clearly communicate the worth of the design beyond aesthetics?"
3. **The Clarity Question**: "Would someone without architectural training understand what they're seeing?"

If you can't answer all three questions positively, the visualization requires refinement before presentation.

Visualization Credibility Markers

Clients assess the credibility of visualizations through subtle cues that many architects overlook:

- **Appropriate Human Presence** - People who resemble the client or their target users
- **Authentic Material Representation** - Materials shown as they actually appear in use
- **Environmental Authenticity** - Lighting and context that match reality
- **Detail Consistency** - Maintaining the same level of detail throughout

When these elements are misaligned, clients sense something is "off" even if they can't articulate what it is, creating subconscious doubt about the entire proposal.

Chapter Summary:

Client-Centered Visualization

The most powerful visualizations aren't necessarily the most technically impressive or artistically stunning—they're the ones that most effectively bridge the gap between architectural thinking and client perception.

By prioritizing emotional connection, demonstrating value, and ensuring clarity, your visualizations become powerful tools for winning projects rather than mere representations of design intent.

Next Client Meeting Action Steps:

1. Review your standard visualization package and evaluate it through the client's eyes
2. Identify opportunities to incorporate emotional and value layers
3. Test visualizations with non-architects before client presentation
4. Structure presentations to follow the client's hierarchy of perception

Chapter 2

From Concept to Commitment

The Visualization Journey

Architectural visualization isn't a single event—it's a strategic sequence that guides clients from initial interest to project commitment. Understanding the psychological progression clients experience allows you to craft visualizations that move them toward the decision.

The client journey typically follows these stages:

1. **Possibility** - "Could this work for me?"
2. **Personalization** - "How would this apply to my specific situation?"
3. **Practical Assessment** - "Will this solve my problems?"
4. **Value Confirmation** - "Is this worth the investment?"
5. **Confidence** - "Is this the right team to execute?"
6. **Commitment** - "I'm ready to proceed"

Each stage requires different visualization approaches. Misalignment between the visualization type and client stage is a primary reason presentations fail to convert to projects.

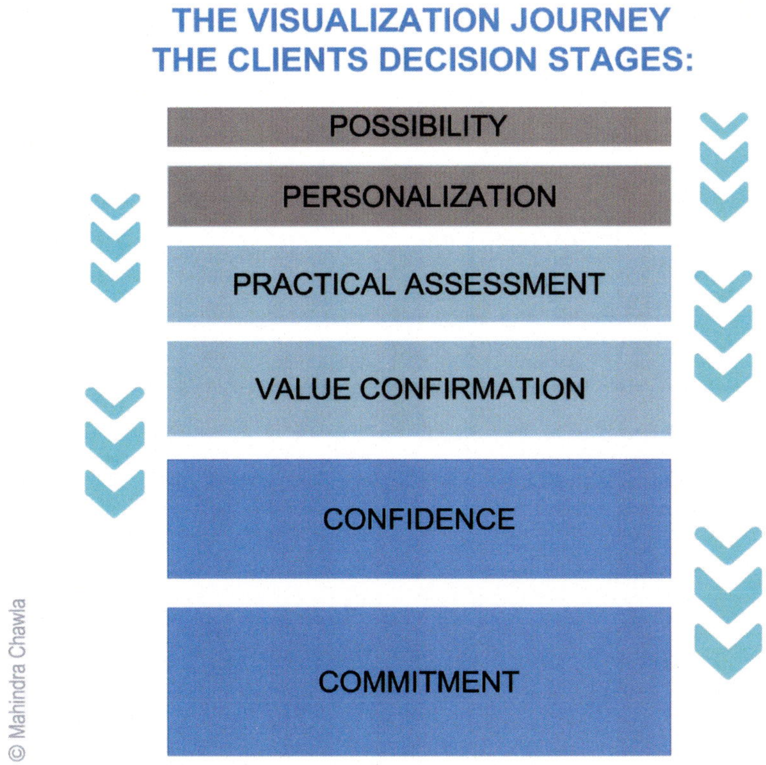

THE CLIENT'S JOURNEY
FROM INITIAL INTEREST TO PROJECT COMMITMENT

Stage-Appropriate Visualization

Stage 1: Possibility Visualization.

At this early stage, clients need to see potential rather than specifics. Effective visualizations at this stage:

- Remain somewhat conceptual rather than highly detailed
- Show range rather than commitment to a single approach
- Connect emotionally to client aspirations
- Avoid overwhelming technical information

Case Example: For a corporate office in Bandra, initial visualizations showed three distinct ceiling treatment concepts in the reception area—not as technical drawings but as experiential views. This allowed the client to react to possibilities without feeling pressured to commit to details.

Stage 2: Personalization Visualization

As clients begin to imagine themselves in the project, visualizations should:

- Incorporate the client-specific elements (brand colours, family photos)
- Present the design in contexts relevant to the client's life or business
- Show the space in use for client-specific activities
- Begin adding more realistic details

Stage 3: Practical Assessment Visualization

Now the clients evaluate functionality. Effective visualizations at this stage:

- Demonstrate solutions to specific client problems
- Show the design handling real-world scenarios
- Include practical details like storage, traffic flow, and adaptability
- Address the expressed concerns through visual solutions

Stage 4: Value Confirmation Visualization

Before committing resources, clients need to confirm value. Visualizations should:

- Highlight quality differences that justify investment
- Demonstrate durability and longevity
- Show difficult-to-achieve details that separate your work
- Present comparative elements (before/after, standard/premium)

Stage 5: Confidence Visualization

Clients now need reassurance about execution. Effective visualizations:

- Include technical details that demonstrate expertise
- Show implementation planning and attention to detail
- Present the past project progression from visualization to completion

- Address potential complications before they become concerns

Stage 6: Commitment Visualization

Finally, as clients prepare to commit, provide visualizations that:

- Incorporate refinements based on client feedback
- Show the finished project in celebratory contexts
- Include a timeline visualization of project progression
- Present the project as already successful

STAGE-APPROPRIATE VISUALIZATION

STAGE	VISUALIZATION FOCUS	KEY ELEMENTS	COMMON MISTAKES
Stage 1: Possibility	Conceptual Potential	• Emotional connection • Range of approaches • Inspirational rather than technical • Shows potential, not specifics	• Too much detail too soon • Technical drawings instead of concepts • Single solution vs. multiple possibilities • Overwhelming with information
Stage 2: Personalization	Client-Specific Adaptation	• Client brand colors/preferences • Family photos or personal elements • Spaces shown in client's context • Activities specific to client's life	• Generic people in visualizations • Ignoring stated preferences • Standard furniture vs. client's style • Missing cultural considerations
Stage 3: Practical Assessment	Functional Problem-Solving	• Solutions to stated problems • Workflow demonstrations • Storage and practical elements • Traffic flow patterns	• Beautiful but impractical solutions • Ignoring functional requirements • Missing accessibility considerations • Overlooking daily use patterns
Stage 4: Value Confirmation	Investment Justification	• Quality differences highlighted • Durability demonstrations • Before/after comparisons • Premium vs. standard options	• Failing to show value differentiation • Missing long-term benefits • Not addressing budget concerns • Unclear return on investment
Stage 5: Confidence	Execution Assurance	• Technical details visible • Past project examples • Implementation planning • Quality control measures	• Vague execution plans • No evidence of past success • Missing technical competence • Unrealistic timelines
Stage 6: Commitment	Final Decision Support	• All client feedback incorporated • Celebration of project success • Timeline visualization • Next steps clearly outlined	• Rushing to close • Missing final refinements • Unclear next steps • No celebration of decision

ALIGNING 'VISUALIZATION APPROACH' WITH THE 'CLIENTS DECISION STAGE' MAXIMIZES CONVERSION POTENTIAL

The Sequencing Strategy

Most architects present all visualization types simultaneously, creating information overload and confusion. Instead, sequence your presentations to match the client's decision journey.

For example, in a residential project presentation:

- Initial meeting: Conceptual visualizations showing the possibility
- Second meeting: Personalized visualizations reflecting client feedback
- Third meeting: Detailed visualizations addressing practical concerns
- Final presentation: Comprehensive visualization package with execution details

This sequencing creates a natural progression toward commitment that feels organic rather than pressured.

Managing the Reality Gap

All visualizations create expectations. The gap between visualization and final reality represents one of the greatest risks in client relationships.

To manage this gap effectively:

1. **Calibrate Visualization Realism** - More photorealistic visualizations create higher expectations
2. **Include Reality Markers** - Elements that clearly won't be idealized in the final project
3. **Visualization Disclaimers** - Clear communication about representational elements

4. **Expectation Management** - Explicit discussion about which elements may vary

The most successful practitioners don't necessarily create the most beautiful visualizations—they create the most honest ones. This builds trust that converts not just to current projects but to long-term client relationships and referrals.

Chapter Summary:

Strategic Visualization Sequencing

By understanding the client's psychological journey and aligning your visualization approach to each stage, you transform visualization from a presentation tool to a conversion strategy.

The most effective visualization approach isn't presenting all information at once, but rather providing the right visualization at the right time to move clients confidently toward commitment.

Next Client Meeting Action Steps:

1. Identify which decision stage your client currently occupies
2. Prepare visualizations appropriate to that stage and the next
3. Structure your presentation as a journey rather than a complete information dump
4. Include clear next steps that naturally follow from your visualization sequence

Chapter 3

Residential Visualization Mastery

The Personal Connection

Residential projects hold a unique position in architectural practice—they are simultaneously the most personal for clients and often the most challenging to visualize effectively. Unlike corporate clients who may have experience with architectural presentations, residential clients are making deeply personal decisions about spaces they'll live in daily.

In my decades of high-end residential work across Mumbai, Bangalore, and beyond, I've found that residential visualization requires a fundamentally different approach than other project types.

The Emotional Hierarchy of Home

When visualizing residential spaces, understand that clients assess designs through this hierarchy:

1. **Identity Reflection** - "Does this space reflect who I am/aspire to be?"
2. **Family Functionality** - "Will this work for how we live?"
3. **Social Impression** - "What will others think when they visit?"
4. **Investment Value** - "Will this maintain or increase property value?"
5. **Aesthetic Appeal** - "Is this beautiful by my standards?"

Notice how technical excellence and design innovation—often architects' primary concerns—don't appear on this list. For most clients, these are assumed but not primary evaluation criteria.

EMOTIONAL HIERARCHY OF A HOME

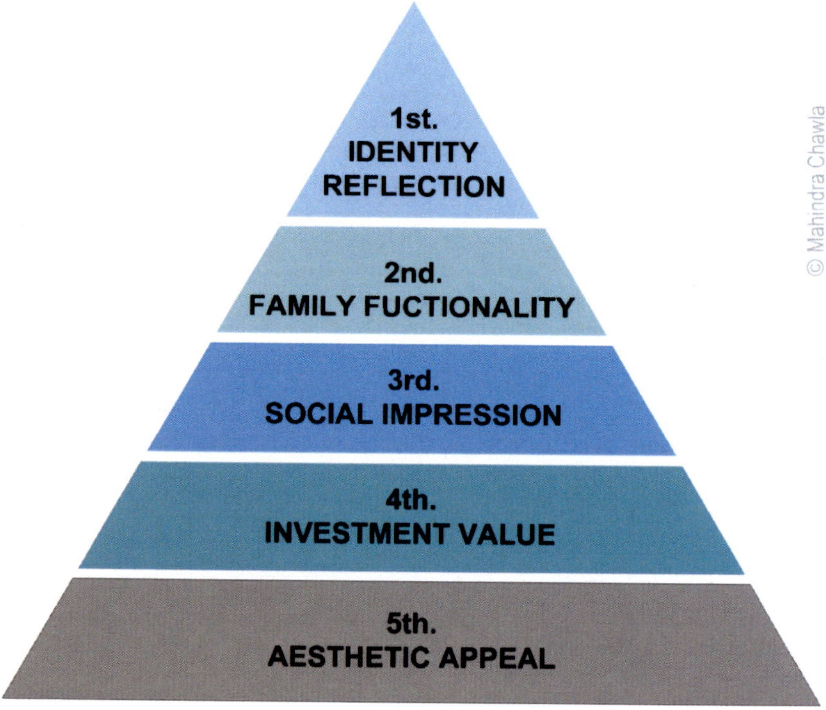

WHAT RESIDENTIAL CLIENTS TRUELY EVALUATE

The Day-in-the-Life Visualization Method

Rather than showing isolated spaces, the most compelling residential visualizations tell the story of life within the home. This approach has been particularly effective for our high-end residential projects in Bandra and Powai.

The method works as follows:

1. **Select 3-5 Key Daily Moments** based on client lifestyle:
    - Morning routine
    - Family gathering times
    - Entertainment scenarios
    - Work-from-home situations
    - Evening relaxation
2. **Create Connected Visualizations** showing the home during these specific moments, with appropriate:
    - Time-of-day lighting
    - Realistic occupancy
    - Actual activities
    - Seasonal considerations
3. **Include Transitional Spaces,** often overlooked in traditional visualization:
    - Entries and thresholds
    - Circulation paths
    - Connections between indoor/outdoor spaces

Case Example: For a family residence in Lonavala, rather than presenting standard room-by-room renderings, we created a visual narrative following a weekend day: morning coffee on the east-facing veranda, afternoon family gathering in the kitchen, evening entertainment in the living area transitioning to the garden, and night-time retreat in the master suite. The clients immediately connected with this approach, saying, "We can see ourselves living here."

THE DAY-IN-THE-LIFE, VISUALIZATION METHOD

MORNING ROUTINE

FAMILY GATHERING

EVENING SCENARIO

EVENING RELAXATION

CONNECTING VISUALIZATION TO DAILY LIFE MOMENTS CREATES EMOTIONAL RESONANCE

Material Authenticity in Residential Visualization

One of the most common disconnects in residential projects occurs when materials appear different in visualization than in reality. This creates disappointment and damages trust. Effective residential visualization requires meticulous attention to material representation.

The authenticity checklist includes:

- **Accurate Reflectivity** - Particularly for marble, metals, and glass
- **Realistic Textile Representation** - Showing proper drape and texture
- **Material Aging Indication** - How materials will weather and patina
- **Contextual Lighting Effects** - How Mumbai's particular light affects materials
- **Scale Accuracy** - Especially for patterns and textures

My recommendation: maintain a physical material library alongside digital assets. Before finalizing any visualization, compare the digital representation with physical samples under similar lighting conditions.

The Family Test

Before presenting residential visualizations to clients, subject them to what I call "The Family Test." This simple but powerful method involves asking these questions:

1. "Would this space comfortably accommodate the specific family members?"
2. "Are the daily patterns of this particular family visible in the visualization?"
3. "Does the visualization reflect the family's cultural and social preferences?"
4. "Are the clients' actual belongings (or reasonable facsimiles) present?"
5. "Does the visualization account for the family's growth and change over time?"

Visualizations that pass this test connect with clients at a fundamental level because they see themselves, not generic occupants, in the space.

Cultural Context in Residential Visualization

Mumbai's residential design requires particular attention to cultural elements that may not be emphasized in Western visualization approaches. Successful residential visualizations in our context often include:

- **Multi-generational Living Considerations** - Spaces for extended family
- **Cultural Celebration Spaces** - Areas for festivals and gatherings
- **Spiritual Spaces** - Puja rooms and meditation areas

- **Indoor-Outdoor Transitions** - Particularly important given our climate
- **Staff Accommodation** - Sensitively integrated service spaces

When these elements are thoughtfully incorporated into visualizations, clients immediately recognize that the design understands their actual living patterns, not just aesthetic preferences.

Visualization for Different Residential Client Types

After hundreds of residential projects, I've identified four primary client archetypes, each requiring different visualization approaches:

The Lifestyle Client

- Prioritizes: Social spaces, entertainment areas, status elements
- Effective approach: Emphasize experiential quality and impression
- Visualization focus: Evening entertainment scenarios, guest experiences

The Family-Centered Client

- Prioritizes: Functionality, growth adaptation, safety, togetherness
- Effective approach: Show spaces in use by family members
- Visualization focus: Daily routines, adaptability, connection between spaces

The Investment-Minded Client

- Prioritizes: Durability, value appreciation, market appeal
- Effective approach: Comparative views and quality differentiation
- Visualization focus: Quality details, timeless elements, maintenance aspects

The Design Enthusiast

- Prioritizes: Innovation, uniqueness, design integrity
- Effective approach: Show design principles and conceptual foundations
- Visualization focus: Design details, material relationships, light quality

Identifying your client type early allows you to tailor visualizations to their specific decision-making framework.

Chapter Summary:

Residential Visualization That Connects

The most successful residential visualizations don't just show houses—they tell the story of a specific family's life within a home. By focusing on authentic material representation, cultural context, daily living patterns, and client-specific priorities, you create visualizations that form an emotional bridge between architectural concept and client commitment.

Next Client Meeting Action Steps:

1. Gather specific information about the client's daily routines before creating visualizations
2. Select 3-5 key moments to visualize rather than covering every space
3. Incorporate actual client possessions or reasonable substitutes
4. Test visualizations against the specific client archetype's priorities

Chapter 4

Corporate Identity Through Space

Beyond Aesthetics to Brand Architecture

Corporate projects present a unique visualization challenge: they must communicate not just design but how the space embodies and advances a company's brand, culture, and business objectives. This chapter draws from our extensive corporate experience across Mumbai, Bangalore, and beyond to provide a framework for visualizations that win corporate projects.

The Stakeholder Complexity Challenge

Unlike residential projects with relatively few decision-makers, corporate projects typically involve multiple stakeholders with different priorities:

- **Leadership** - Concerned with brand representation and impression
- **Finance** - Focused on budget efficiency and long-term value
- **Operations** - Prioritizing functionality and workflow
- **HR** - Interested in employee experience and culture support
- **Facilities** - Focused on maintenance and adaptability

Effective corporate visualization must address all these stakeholders simultaneously or risk project derailment. This requires a multi-layered approach I call "Stakeholder-Conscious Visualization."

STAKEHOLDER -CONSCIOUS VISUALIZATION

STAKE HOLDER	FACILITIES	HUMAN RESOURCES	OPERATIONS	FINANCE	LEADERSHIP
PRIMARY CONCERN	MAINTENANCE AND LONG-TERM ADAPTABILITY	EMPLOYEE EXPERIENCE AND CULTURE SUPPORT	FUNCTIONALITY AND WORKFLOW OPTIMIZATION	BUDGET EFFICIENCY AND LONG-TERM VALUE	BRAND REPRESENTATION AND IMPRESSION
VISUALIZATION FOCUS	BUILDING SYSTEMS AND OPERATIONAL EASE	COLLABORATION AND WELLBEING SPACES	DAILY OPERATIONS AND PROCESS FLOW	COST OPTIMIZATION AND ROI DEMONSTRATION	CLIENT-FACING AREAS AND BRAND MOMENTS
KEY ELEMENTS TO INCLUDE	• ACCESS FOR MAINTENANCE AND REPAIRS • MODULAR SYSTEMS FOR FUTURE CHANGES • QUALITY OF MATERIALS AND SYSTEMS • CLEAR SERVICE AND UTILITY AREAS • FLEXIBLE INFRASTRUCTURE FOR TECHNOLOGY	• DIVERSE WORK SETTINGS FOR DIFFERENT TASKS • SOCIAL AND BREAK AREAS • NATURAL LIGHT AND ERGONOMIC CONSIDERATIONS • FLEXIBLE SPACES FOR TEAM ACTIVITIES • QUIET ZONES FOR FOCUSED WORK	• WORKFLOW DIAGRAMS AND CIRCULATION PATHS • DEPARTMENT ADJACENCIES • STORAGE AND UTILITY REQUIREMENTS • TECHNOLOGY INTEGRATION POINTS • MAINTENANCE ACCESSIBILITY	• SPACE UTILIZATION METRICS • BEFORE/AFTER EFFICIENCY COMPARISONS • DURABLE, LOW-MAINTENANCE MATERIALS • ENERGY EFFICIENCY FEATURES • FUTURE ADAPTABILITY TO AVOID RENOVATIONS	• RECEPTION AND ENTRANCE AREAS • EXECUTIVE MEETING ROOMS • BRAND TOUCHPOINTS AND SIGNAGE • PREMIUM MATERIALS AND FINISHES • SPACES THAT REFLECT COMPANY STATUS

ADDRESSING MULTIPLE CORPORATE STAKEHOLDERS THROUGH TARGETED VISUALIZATION ENSURES PROJECT APPROVAL AND IMPLEMENTATION SUCCESS

The Brand Translation Method

The most successful corporate visualizations begin not with design concepts but with brand translation—the process of identifying how a company's values and identity manifest in physical space.

The method works as follows:

1. **Identify 3-5 Core Brand Values** through client consultation. Example: Innovation, Collaboration, Transparency, Client-Focus
2. **Translate Each Value to Spatial Characteristics** Example: "Transparency" might translate to visual connections between departments, clear wayfinding, and literal transparency through glass partitions
3. **Create Visualizations That Explicitly Connect Values to Design** Using side-by-side presentation of value statements and their spatial manifestations

Case Example: For a technology company's headquarters in Andheri East, we created visualization pairs—each showing a key brand value and its spatial expression. For "Innovation," we visualized both traditional meeting spaces and informal collaboration areas, demonstrating how the design supported multiple work modes. This approach allowed non-design executives to evaluate the proposal based on business criteria, not just design aesthetics.

BRAND TRANSLATION METHOD

Brand Value example: TRANSPARENCY
Spatial Characteristic:
VISUAL CONNECTS BETWEEN DEPARTMENTS
Visualization Approach:
SHOW SIGHT LINES & OPEN CONNECTIONS

Brand Value example: COLLABORATION
Spatial Characteristic:
CENTRAL GATHERING SPACES WITH TECHNOLOGY INTEGRATION
Visualization Approach:
SHOW PEOPLE INTERACTING IN VARIOUS GROUP SIZES

Workflow Visualization

Corporate clients need to see not just how spaces look but how they function. Workflow visualization demonstrates operational efficiency through:

- **User Journey Mapping** - Visualizing how different employees move through the space
- **Adjacency Optimization** - Showing how related functions are positioned
- **Flexibility Demonstration** - Visualizing how spaces adapt to different needs
- **Technology Integration** - Showing how digital and physical environments merge

The most effective technique combines static visualizations with simple animated sequences showing space in use during typical workflows.

The ROI Visualization Framework

Corporate clients make decisions based on return on investment. Effective visualizations must make this ROI visible by showing:

1. **Efficiency Gains** - How the design optimizes space utilization
2. **Experience Enhancement** - How the design improves employee and client experience
3. **Brand Alignment** - How the design reinforces brand perception
4. **Adaptability Value** - How the design accommodates future changes

5. **Talent Attraction** - How the design serves as a recruitment and retention tool

Case Example: For a financial services firm in BKC, we created a split-screen visualization showing current versus proposed spaces with key metrics overlaid: seating capacity, meeting room availability, natural light exposure, and collaboration space allocation. This data-enhanced visualization secured budget approval because it demonstrated quantifiable improvements, not just aesthetic upgrades.

Visualization for Different Corporate Client Types

Corporate clients generally fall into four archetypes, each requiring different visualization emphasis:

The Image-Conscious Corporation

- Prioritizes: Client impression, brand projection, market positioning
- Effective approach: Emphasize reception, client-facing areas, brand moments
- Visualization focus: Client journey, brand touchpoints, memorable features

The Efficiency-Driven Corporation

- Prioritizes: Space optimization, workflow enhancement, operational improvement
- Effective approach: Demonstrate space efficiency and functional gains
- Visualization focus: Before/after comparisons, density plans, flow diagrams

The Culture-Focused Corporation

- Prioritizes: Employee experience, collaboration, wellbeing, retention
- Effective approach: Show spaces in use by employees in various scenarios
- Visualization focus: Collaboration areas, amenities, adaptability to different work modes

The Innovation-Seeking Corporation

- Prioritizes: Cutting-edge solutions, technology integration, future-readiness
- Effective approach: Highlight innovative features and adaptability
- Visualization focus: Technology integration, unique solutions, forward-looking elements

Identifying your corporate client's archetype allows for targeted visualization that speaks directly to their primary concerns.

Phasing and Implementation Visualization

Corporate projects often require phased implementation to maintain business operations. Effective visualizations must address this complexity through:

- **Phasing Diagrams** - Visual timelines of implementation stages
- **Disruption Minimization** - Showing how work continues during construction
- **Temporary Conditions** - Visualizing interim states during phased implementation

- **Critical Path Highlights** - Identifying key milestones visually

This approach demonstrates not just design excellence but implementation intelligence—a crucial factor in corporate decision-making.

Cultural Sensitivity in Global Corporate Visualization

For multinational corporations, visualizations must respect cultural variations while maintaining brand consistency. Key considerations include:

- **Local Work Patterns** - How regional offices may function differently
- **Cultural Space Requirements** - Different needs for personal space, meeting areas
- **Regional Material Appropriateness** - What works in Mumbai vs. Delhi vs. Bangalore
- **Local Environmental Considerations** - Climate adaptation and sustainability

The most effective global corporate visualizations demonstrate both brand consistency and cultural adaptability.

Chapter Summary:

Strategic Corporate Visualization

Winning corporate projects requires visualization that speaks the language of business as fluently as the language of design. By focusing on brand alignment, operational efficiency, stakeholder needs, and implementation intelligence, you create visualizations that demonstrate what the space will look like and how it will advance the client's business objectives.

Next Client Meeting Action Steps:

1. Identify key stakeholders and their specific concerns before creating visualizations
2. Translate stated business goals and brand values into spatial concepts
3. Include operational metrics alongside aesthetic presentations
4. Prepare different visualization emphasis for different stakeholder presentations

Chapter 5

Visualization for Renovation and Structural Repair

Revealing Hidden Potential

Renovation and structural repair projects present unique visualization challenges. Unlike new construction, these projects require communicating both existing conditions and transformation potential. Drawing from our structural repair experiences with projects like the BAGD School in Chembur and various residential buildings in Mumbai, this chapter reveals strategies for visualizations that win renovation projects.

The Credibility Challenge

Renovation visualization faces a fundamental credibility hurdle: clients can see the current reality and will directly compare your visualization against it. Any disconnect creates immediate doubt. This requires a different approach than new construction visualization.

The four principles of credible renovation visualization:

1. **Accurate Existing Conditions Documentation**
2. **Reality-Anchored Transformation**
3. **Technical Confidence Building**
4. **Value Demonstration**

Let's examine each principle in practice.

Documenting the Present to Visualize the Future

Effective renovation visualization begins with meticulous documentation of existing conditions:

- **Photo-Documentation Integration** - Incorporating actual site photography
- **Condition Mapping** - Visually identifying structural and aesthetic issues
- **Constraint Identification** - Honestly acknowledging limitations
- **Historical Context Preservation** - Recognizing heritage value

Case Example: For the 1950s residential building in Mumbai, we began with comprehensive photographic documentation, creating a detailed condition assessment visualization that color-coded structural issues, aesthetic concerns, and historical elements. This demonstrated our thorough understanding of the building before proposing changes, establishing immediate credibility with the landlady.

The Transformation Continuum Method

Rather than showing only "before" and "after," effective renovation visualization presents a transformation continuum that might include:

1. **Existing Conditions** - Accurately documented current state
2. **Structural Remediation** - Technical repair visualization
3. **Functional Improvement** - Operational enhancements
4. **Aesthetic Transformation** - Final design vision

5. **Future Adaptability** - Long-term potential

This approach helps clients understand the logical progression and necessity of each stage, supporting budget justification for comprehensive renovation rather than superficial fixes.

THE TRANSFORMATION CONTINUUM

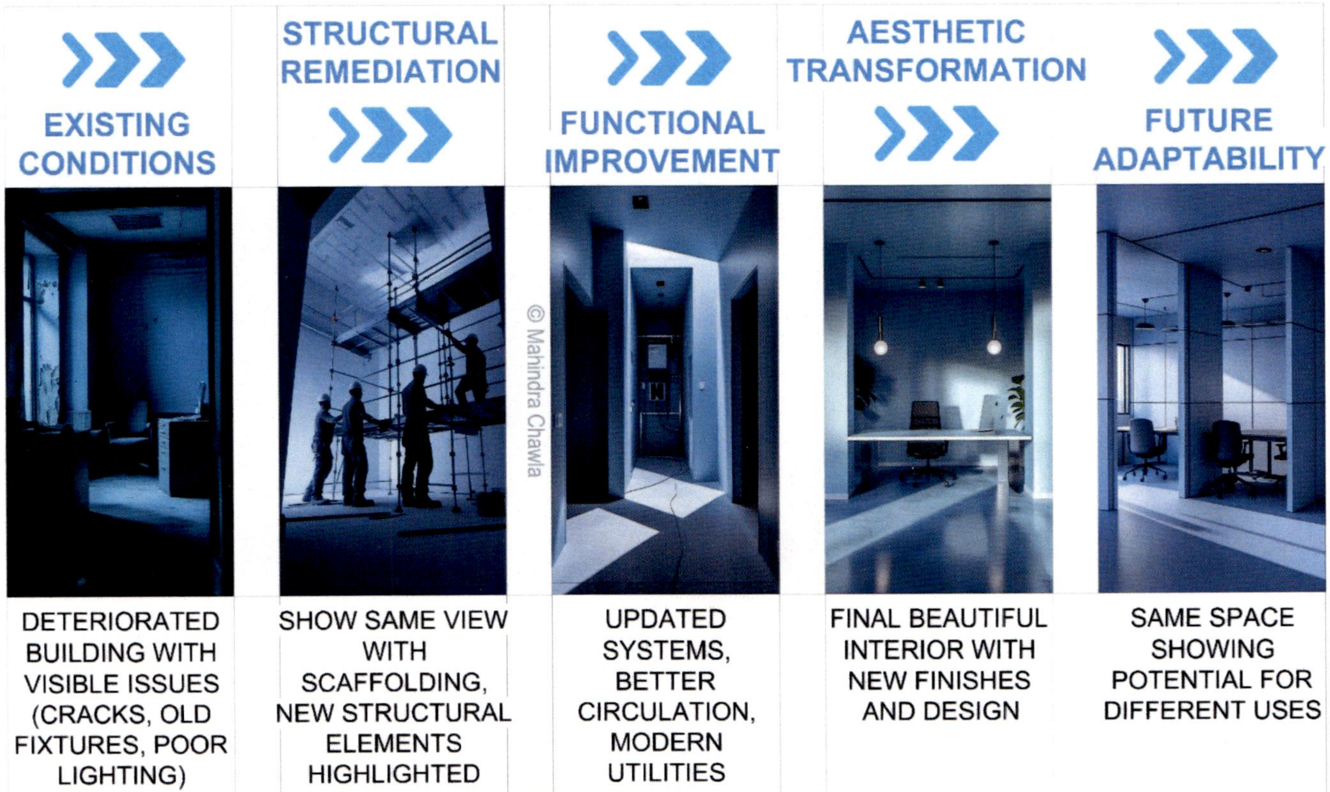

Technical Confidence Visualization

Renovation and repair projects require particular attention to technical visualization that builds client confidence:

- **Structural System Exposure** - Visualizing normally hidden elements
- **Problem-Solution Pairing** - Directly connecting issues to remedies
- **Methodological Transparency** - Showing how repairs will be executed
- **Risk Mitigation Representation** - Demonstrating safety and contingency planning

VISUALIZATION ELEMENT	PURPOSE	CLIENT IMPACT	EXAMPLE APPLICATION
STRUCTURAL SYSTEM EXPOSURE	REVEALS HIDDEN CONDITIONS AND PROPOSED SOLUTIONS	DEMONSTRATES THOROUGHNESS AND TECHNICAL UNDERSTANDING	
PROBLEM-SOLUTION PAIRING	CONNECTS SPECIFIC ISSUES TO TARGETED REMEDIES	BUILDS METHODOLOGICAL CONFIDENCE AND JUSTIFIES COSTS	
METHODOLOGICAL TRANSPARENCY	SHOWS STEP-BY-STEP REPAIR EXECUTION	PROVES SYSTEMATIC APPROACH AND REDUCES UNCERTAINTY	
RISK MITIGATION REPRESENTATION	DEMONSTRATES SAFETY AND CONTINGENCY PLANNING	ASSURES CLIENTS OF PROFESSIONAL RISK MANAGEMENT	
ACCESS AND LOGISTICS PLANNING	SHOWS HOW WORK WILL BE EXECUTED IN OCCUPIED BUILDINGS	REDUCES CLIENT ANXIETY ABOUT DISRUPTION	
QUALITY CONTROL INDICATORS	HIGHLIGHTS INSPECTION POINTS AND STANDARDS	BUILDS CONFIDENCE IN EXECUTION EXCELLENCE	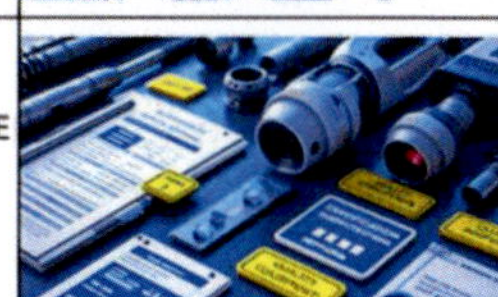
TIMELINE INTEGRATION	CONNECTS TECHNICAL WORK TO PROJECT SCHEDULE	MANAGES EXPECTATIONS AND SHOWS EFFICIENCY	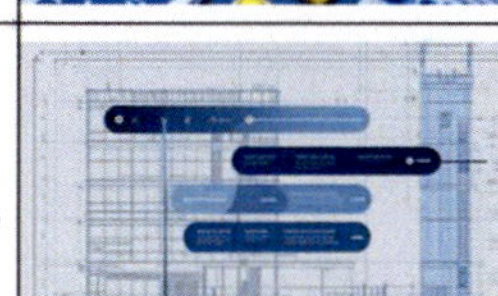
CODE COMPLIANCE VISUALIZATION	SHOWS ADHERENCE TO BUILDING REGULATIONS	DEMONSTRATES LEGAL AND SAFETY COMPLIANCE	

Case Example: For the BAGD School structural repair project in Chembur, we created sectional visualizations showing both the deteriorated structural conditions and the proposed reinforcement methods. Though not aesthetically focused, these technical visualizations were crucial in securing the project because they demonstrated methodological expertise and safety consciousness essential for a school renovation.

The Phasing Clarity Imperative

Renovation projects typically require occupants to remain in place during work. Effective visualization must address this reality through:

- **Phasing Diagrams** - Clear visual sequencing of work
- **Disruption Mapping** - Honest representation of impact on occupants
- **Temporary Condition Visualization** - Showing interim states
- **Daily Life Continuity** - Demonstrating how normal activities continue

Clients appreciate this honesty more than unrealistic promises of disruption-free renovation, as it builds trust and allows for proper expectations.

Value-Enhancement Visualization

The most persuasive renovation visualizations clearly demonstrate value enhancement through:

1. **Problem-Resolution Pairs** - Showing specific issues and their solutions
2. **Functional Improvement Metrics** - Quantifying operational benefits
3. **Aesthetic Transformation Highlights** - Showcasing design improvements
4. **Sustainability Enhancements** - Demonstrating efficiency gains
5. **Longevity Visualization** - Showing extended building lifespan

Case Example: For the actor's office renovation in Andheri East, we created a multi-layered visualization showing not just aesthetic improvements but also workflow enhancements, technology integration, and energy efficiency gains. By quantifying these benefits, we demonstrated a clear return on investment beyond mere appearance upgrades.

Cultural and Heritage Sensitivity

Mumbai's architectural landscape contains significant heritage value. Renovation visualization must respect this through:

- **Character-Defining Element Identification** - Highlighting important historical features
- **Preservation-Enhancement Balance** - Showing how history and modernization coexist

- **Contextual Harmony** - Demonstrating neighbourhood compatibility
- **Narrative Continuity** - Connecting the building history to its future

This approach particularly resonates with clients who value the historical and cultural significance of their properties while desiring modern functionality.

Visualization for Different Renovation Client Types

Based on our extensive renovation experience, we've identified four primary renovation client archetypes:

The Problem-Solver

- Primary concern: Addressing specific functional or structural issues
- Effective approach: Technical visualization focusing on solutions to identified problems
- Visualization emphasis: Before/after comparisons highlighting resolution of specific concerns

The Value-Enhancer

- Primary concern: Increasing property value or utility
- Effective approach: ROI-focused visualization demonstrating tangible improvements
- Visualization emphasis: Market comparison, efficiency gains, modernization benefits

The Preserver

- Primary concern: Maintaining historical or emotional significance
- Effective approach: Heritage-sensitive visualization showing respectful intervention
- Visualization emphasis: Preservation of character-defining elements, historical continuity

The Transformer

- Primary concern: Creating dramatic change while leveraging the existing structure
- Effective approach: Vision-oriented visualization showing bold transformation
- Visualization emphasis: Contrast between existing and proposed, innovative reuse

Identifying your renovation client's archetype allows you to tailor the visualization that addresses their specific priorities.

Structural Repair Visualization Specifics

Structural repair presents unique visualization challenges because the most important work is often invisible in the final product. Effective structural repair visualization:

- **Makes the Invisible Visible** - Reveals normally concealed structural elements
- **Uses Cutaway Techniques** - Shows intervention within existing structures
- **Employs Sequential Logic** - Demonstrates step-by-step repair methodology
- **Incorporates Technical Authority** - Includes engineering details that build confidence

For the Hibiscus Co-op Housing Society repair project, our visualization included transparent overlays showing the existing structure, damage assessment, intervention method, and final appearance. This comprehensive approach secured the project despite a slightly higher bid than competitors because it demonstrated superior technical understanding.

Chapter Summary:

Renovation Visualization That Builds Trust

Successful renovation and repair visualization requires balancing technical accuracy with transformation vision. By documenting existing conditions thoroughly, demonstrating methodical solutions, addressing phasing realities, and highlighting value enhancement, you create visualizations that build the trust necessary for renovation projects.

Next Client Meeting Action Steps:

1. Conduct thorough site documentation before creating any transformation visualizations
2. Create visualizations that show the logical progression from problems to solutions
3. Incorporate technical details that build confidence in your methodology
4. Balance preservation and transformation based on client archetype

Chapter 6

Building Your Visualization Signature

Standing Out in a Competitive Market

In today's architecture and design landscape, technical visualization skills are increasingly commoditized. What separates successful practices is not just visualization ability but a distinctive visualization approach—a signature style that clients recognize and value. This chapter explores how to develop your unique visualization voice based on over thirty years of practice evolution.

Beyond Technical Excellence: The Recognition Factor

Clients rarely select architects based solely on technical excellence. They choose practices whose work they recognize and connect with emotionally. Your visualization signature is a powerful tool for creating this recognition and connection.

The four elements of a compelling visualization signature:

1. **Consistent Visual Language** - Recognizable approaches across projects
2. **Value Emphasis** - What your visualizations consistently highlight
3. **Emotional Tone** - The feelings your visualizations evoke
4. **Technical Distinction** - Your unique approach to visualization challenges

Finding Your Authentic Visualization Voice

Your most effective visualization signature emerges from the intersection of:

- **Your Design Values** - What you believe is most important in architecture
- **Your Technical Strengths** - What you execute particularly well
- **Your Client Niche** - The specific clients you serve best
- **Your Market Position** - How you differentiate from competitors

Case Example: Our practice evolved a visualization signature emphasizing the connection between interiors and architecture, highlighting transitional spaces and material relationships at boundaries. This approach emerged naturally from our background spanning both disciplines and differentiated us from practices focused exclusively on either architecture or interiors.

Signature Development Strategy

Developing a recognized visualization signature is an intentional process:

1. **Audit Your Best Work** - Identify common successful elements across projects
2. **Client Feedback Analysis** - Note what clients consistently respond to
3. **Competitive Differentiation** - Assess what distinguishes your approach
4. **Intentional Amplification** - Strengthen these distinctive elements

This doesn't mean creating an artificial style, but identifying and amplifying your authentic strengths.

DEVELOPING A RECOGNISED VISUALIZATION SIGNATURE REQUIRES CONTINUOUS REFINEMENT THROUGH SYSTEMATIC ANALYSIS AND INTENTIONAL STRENGTHENING OF AUTHENTIC SUCCESSFUL ELEMENTS

The Consistency-Flexibility Balance

A successful visualization signature maintains consistency while adapting to project requirements:

- **Core Elements** - Remain consistent across all projects
- **Project-Specific Adaptations** - Flex to meet unique needs
- **Client-Appropriate Variations** - Adjust based on client type
- **Evolution Over Time** - Allow for growth without losing recognition

The strongest signatures are recognizable without being formulaic or rigid.

Case Study: Signature Evolution in Practice

Our signature visualization approach evolved through three distinct phases:

Phase 1: Technical Emphasis (Early 1990s) Initially, we focused on technical accuracy and construction feasibility, reflecting our structural and architectural background. Visualizations emphasized construction detail and practical implementation.

Phase 2: Interior-Architecture Integration (2000s) As our practice expanded into more interior work, our visualization evolved to emphasize the relationship between architectural shell and interior experience. This period saw the development of our "inside-out" visualization approach.

Phase 3: Experience-Centered Visualization (2010s onward) Our current signature focuses on human experience, visualizing spaces through the lens of daily use and emotional response while maintaining our technical foundation and interior-architecture integration.

This evolution was not planned but emerged through consistent reflection on client response and project success.

Visualization Signature Elements to Consider

When developing your signature, consider these potential distinguishing elements:

- **Perspective Choice** - Consistent viewpoint approaches
- **Lighting Character** - Distinctive illumination style
- **Material Representation** - Unique approach to textures and surfaces
- **Human Presence** - How you incorporate people
- **Context Integration** - How you show the relationship to the surroundings
- **Detail Emphasis** - What you consistently highlight
- **Narrative Approach** - How you tell the project story

Your signature might emphasize several of these elements while maintaining flexibility in others.

VISUALIZATION SIGNATURE ELEMENTS

SELECTION MATRIX: BUILDING YOUR DISTINCTIVE VISUALIZATION APPROACH

ELEMENT	DESCRIPTION	SIGNATURE POTENTIAL	EXAMPLE APPLICATIONS	CONSISTENCY LEVEL
PERSPECTIVE CHOICE	CONSISTENT VIEWPOINT APPROACHES AND ANGLE PREFERENCES	⭐⭐⭐⭐⭐	• ALWAYS SHOWING HUMAN-EYE LEVEL VIEWS • EMPHASIS ON ENTRY SEQUENCE PERSPECTIVES • BIRD'S EYE VIEWS FOR SPATIAL RELATIONSHIPS	**CORE ELEMENT, USE IN EVERY PROJECT**
LIGHTING CHARACTER	DISTINCTIVE ILLUMINATION STYLE AND TIME-OF-DAY PREFERENCES	⭐⭐⭐⭐⭐	• GOLDEN HOUR LIGHTING FOR WARMTH • DRAMATIC SHADOWS FOR DEPTH • NATURAL LIGHT PROGRESSION THROUGH THE DAY	**CORE ELEMENT, SIGNATURE LIGHTING MOOD**
MATERIAL REPRESENTATION	UNIQUE APPROACH TO TEXTURES, SURFACES, AND TACTILE QUALITIES	⭐⭐⭐⭐	• HAND-SKETCHED MATERIAL DETAILS • REALISTIC AGING AND PATINA • TACTILE QUALITY EMPHASIS	**STRONG ELEMENT, CONSISTENT APPROACH**
HUMAN PRESENCE	HOW PEOPLE ARE INCORPORATED INTO VISUALIZATIONS	⭐⭐⭐⭐	• REAL FAMILIES VS. GENERIC FIGURES • CULTURAL AUTHENTICITY • ACTIVITY-SPECIFIC OCCUPANCY	**STRONG ELEMENT, CONSISTENT PHILOSOPHY**
CONTEXT INTEGRATION	HOW SURROUNDING ENVIRONMENT IS SHOWN AND EMPHASIZED	⭐⭐⭐	• MUMBAI'S SPECIFIC LIGHT QUALITY • NEIGHBORHOOD CHARACTER INCLUSION • CULTURAL CONTEXT ELEMENTS	**MODERATE ELEMENT, PROJECT-SPECIFIC**
DETAIL EMPHASIS	WHAT ELEMENTS ARE CONSISTENTLY HIGHLIGHTED OR FEATURED	⭐⭐⭐⭐⭐	• TRANSITION SPACES AND THRESHOLDS • MATERIAL CONNECTIONS AND JOINTS • HUMAN-SCALE INTIMATE MOMENTS	**CORE ELEMENT, YOUR UNIQUE FOCUS**
NARRATIVE APPROACH	HOW THE PROJECT STORY IS TOLD THROUGH VISUALIZATION SEQUENCE	⭐⭐⭐⭐	• DAY-IN-THE-LIFE PROGRESSIONS • BEFORE/DURING/AFTER SEQUENCES • PROBLEM-TO-SOLUTION STORYTELLING	**STRONG ELEMENT, CONSISTENT METHODOLOGY**
COLOR PALETTE	SIGNATURE COLOR APPROACHES AND EMOTIONAL TONE	⭐⭐⭐	• WARM, NATURAL COLOR SCHEMES • MUMBAI-SPECIFIC MATERIAL COLORS • SOPHISTICATED, MUTED TONES	**MODERATE ELEMENT, PROJECT-ADAPTABLE**
TECHNICAL INTEGRATION	HOW TECHNICAL INFORMATION IS WOVEN INTO VISUALIZATIONS	⭐⭐⭐⭐	• STRUCTURAL ELEMENTS MADE VISIBLE • CONSTRUCTION METHODOLOGY SHOWN • PROBLEM-SOLVING MADE CLEAR	**STRONG ELEMENT, YOUR EXPERTISE**
EMOTIONAL TONE	CONSISTENT FEELING EVOKED ACROSS ALL VISUALIZATIONS	⭐⭐⭐⭐⭐	• "LIVED-IN" WARMTH VS. STERILE PERFECTION • ASPIRATIONAL YET ACHIEVABLE • PROFESSIONAL YET APPROACHABLE	**CORE ELEMENT, DEFINES YOUR BRAND**

Digital vs. Hand Visualization in Your Signature

In an age of increasingly photorealistic digital visualization, consider whether incorporating hand elements might strengthen your signature:

- **Hybrid Approaches** - Combining digital and hand techniques
- **Conceptual Sketching** - Using hand visualization for early concept communication
- **Detail Highlighting** - Hand-drawn emphasis of key elements
- **Process Transparency** - Showing design evolution through mixed media

Some of our most successful presentations combine digital precision with hand-drawn elements that emphasize the human touch in our design process.

Documenting and Evolving Your Signature

Once identified, document your visualization signature through:

1. **Style Guide Development** - Codify key elements and approaches
2. **Team Training** - Ensure consistency across your practice
3. **Case Examples** - Document successful applications
4. **Evolution Tracking** - Monitor signature development over time

This documentation serves both internal consistency and intentional evolution as your practice grows.

Beyond Visual Style: Philosophical Signature

The most powerful visualization signatures extend beyond visual style to a philosophical approach. Our practice signature includes these philosophical elements:

- **Always showing spaces in use, never empty**
- **Emphasizing transitions between spaces**
- **Demonstrating how natural light changes throughout the day**
- **Revealing the relationship between interior and exterior**
- **Highlighting material connections and transitions**

These philosophical elements provide consistency even when visual style varies across project types.

Signature Development Recommendations:

CORE ELEMENTS (Use in Every Project):

- **Perspective Choice**: Human-centered viewpoints
- **Lighting Character**: Natural, warm illumination
- **Detail Emphasis**: Transitions and human-scale moments
- **Emotional Tone**: Lived-in warmth and authenticity

STRONG ELEMENTS (Consistent Approach):

- **Material Representation**: Realistic, tactile quality
- **Human Presence**: Culturally authentic occupancy
- **Narrative Approach**: Story-driven visualization sequences
- **Technical Integration**: Visible expertise and methodology

MODERATE ELEMENTS (Project-Adaptable):

- **Context Integration**: Location-specific environmental factors
- **Color Palette**: Harmonious but project-appropriate schemes

Your Signature Profile Example:

Based on the Chawla N Associates approach described in the book

"Interior-Architecture Integration Signature"

- **Always show spaces in use, never empty**
- **Emphasize transitions between interior and exterior**
- **Demonstrate natural light changes throughout the day**
- **Reveal material connections and construction logic**
- **Focus on human experience and daily life patterns**

Action Steps for Signature Development:

1. **Select 3-4 Core Elements** that feel most authentic to your approach
2. **Define your approach** for each selected element
3. **Create consistency guidelines** for your team
4. **Document examples** of successful applications
5. **Evolve gradually** while maintaining recognizable elements

"Selecting and consistently applying signature elements creates recognition and differentiation while maintaining flexibility for diverse project requirements."

Chapter Summary:

Cultivating Recognition Through Visualization

Developing a distinctive visualization signature isn't about creating an artificial style—it's about identifying and amplifying the authentic elements that make your approach valuable and recognizable. By consistently expressing your unique perspective through visualization, you create a powerful tool for client connection and practice growth.

Next Client Meeting Action Steps:

1. Review your visualization portfolio to identify recurring successful elements
2. Develop a simple description of your visualization philosophy
3. Ensure new visualizations consciously incorporate signature elements
4. Collect client feedback on what aspects of your visualization approach they find most valuable

Chapter 7

Technology Integration for Client Impact

Practical Innovation in Visualization

Technology is transforming architectural visualization at an unprecedented pace. However, the most successful practitioners focus not on technology for its own sake, but on strategic technology integration that enhances client understanding and drives project decisions. This chapter explores practical technology applications that create genuine client impact.

Beyond Novelty: The Client Value Test

Every visualization technology must pass a simple test: Does it enhance the client's understanding in ways that lead to better decisions? This client-centered approach helps navigate the constantly evolving technology landscape.

The four criteria for effective technology integration:

1. **Accessibility** - Can clients engage with it without special expertise?
2. **Comprehension Enhancement** - Does it improve understanding beyond traditional methods?
3. **Decision Support** - Does it facilitate better, faster client decisions?
4. **Implementation Feasibility** - Can it be reliably delivered within project constraints?

THE CLIENT VALUE TEST:

The Simple 4-Question Framework:

1. Can clients use it easily? (No training needed)
2. Does it make the design clearer? (Better than drawings)
3. Do clients decide faster? (Speeds up choices)
4. Can we do it reliably? (within budget and time)

Decision Rule: All YES = Use it | Any NO = Traditional methods

Strategic Technology Selection

Rather than chasing every new visualization technology, successful practitioners develop a strategic approach to technology adoption:

- **Client-Specific Selection** - Choosing technologies based on client sophistication
- **Project-Appropriate Application** - Matching technology to project complexity
- **Value-Enhancement Focus** - Prioritizing tools that demonstrably improve outcomes
- **Expertise-Aligned Implementation** - Selecting technologies your team can execute well

Case Example: For a high-end residential project in Aamby Valley, we selectively incorporated VR visualization for spatial understanding of complex ceiling geometries while using traditional techniques for other aspects. This targeted application addressed a specific communication challenge rather than attempting a comprehensive VR implementation.

Practical Applications of Current Technologies

Let's examine practical applications of key visualization technologies based on our implementation experience:

Augmented Reality (AR)

- **Most Effective Use**: On-site visualization of proposed changes to existing structures
- **Client Impact**: Helps clients visualize interventions in context
- **Practical Implementation**: Simple AR applications on client devices with pre-placed markers
- **Project Types**: Particularly valuable for renovation and adaptive reuse

Virtual Reality (VR)

- **Most Effective Use**: Spatial experience validation for complex geometries
- **Client Impact**: Provides intuitive spatial understanding beyond 2D representation
- **Practical Implementation**: Targeted VR for specific complex spaces rather than entire projects
- **Project Types**: Most valuable for projects with unconventional spatial relationships

Understanding AR & VR: A Quick Reference Guide

AR (Augmented Reality)

What it is: *Digital information overlaid on the real world through your device's camera*

Simple Example:

- *Point your phone camera at an empty room*
- *See proposed furniture/design changes appear on your screen as if they're there*
- *You still see the actual room, but with digital additions*

For Architecture:

- *Stand in an existing space and see proposed renovations overlaid*
- *View new furniture placement in an empty room*
- *See structural changes on existing buildings*

Common AR Examples You Might Know:

- *Snapchat filters (add digital glasses/hats to your face)*
- *Pokémon Go (digital creatures in real locations)*
- *IKEA app (place virtual furniture in your room)*

VR (Virtual Reality)

What it is: *A completely artificial digital environment that replaces what you see*

Simple Example:

- *Put on special goggles/headset*
- *Everything you see is computer-generated*
- *You're "transported" to a different place entirely*
- *Can walk around and explore the digital space*

For Architecture:

- *"Walk through" a building before it's built*
- *Experience different design options in full 3D*
- *Feel the scale and proportions of spaces*

Common VR Examples You Might Know:

- *Gaming headsets (PlayStation VR, Oculus)*
- *Virtual tours of distant places*
- *Training simulations*

Key Difference:

- ***AR**: Real world + digital additions (mixed reality)*
- ***VR**: Complete digital replacement of reality*

Both can help clients understand architectural designs better than traditional drawings, but they must pass your "Client Value Test" - they should be accessible, enhance understanding, support decisions, and be feasible to implement.

For most projects, simple AR on smartphones might be more practical than expensive VR setups.

Real-Time Rendering

- **Most Effective Use**: Interactive option exploration during client meetings
- **Client Impact**: Facilitates immediate feedback and adaptation
- **Practical Implementation**: Prepare limited variables for modification during presentations
- **Project Types**: Effective for projects where client co-creation is important

AI-Enhanced Visualization

- **Most Effective Use**: Rapid iteration of design alternatives
- **Client Impact**: Provides broader exploration of possibilities
- **Practical Implementation**: Use AI to generate options, then refine with traditional methods
- **Project Types**: Early-stage concept development across project types

The Technology-Trust Balance

While technology can enhance visualization, it also introduces new trust challenges:

- **Expectation Management** - Ensuring visualizations don't promise what can't be delivered
- **Technical Transparency** - Being clear about what is represented vs. simulated
- **Reality Calibration** - Including elements that ground technology in recognizable reality
- **Appropriate Realism** - Matching visualization fidelity to project development stage

The most successful technology integration maintains trust while enhancing understanding.

Low-Tech/High-Impact Approaches

Sometimes the most effective "technology" is surprisingly simple:

- **Physical/Digital Hybrids** - Combining digital visualization with physical models
- **Sequential Reveal Techniques** - Layered presentation methods showing progressive development
- **Comparative Visualization** - Simple side-by-side comparisons of options
- **Annotation Enhancement** - Adding interactive explanatory elements to traditional visualization

Case Example: For a complex corporate office renovation in Mumbai, we created a hybrid presentation combining digital visualizations with a physical layer model that clients could manipulate. This approach proved more effective than fully immersive technology because it allowed intuitive group interaction and decision-making.

Implementation Strategy for Different Practice Sizes

Technology implementation varies based on practice scale:

Small Practices (1-5 People)

- Focus on accessible technologies with low implementation barriers
- Consider subscription services rather than significant capital investment
- Develop partnerships with specialized visualization consultants
- Prioritize technologies with broad application across your project types

Mid-Size Practices (6-20 People)

- Develop internal expertise in 1-2 strategic technologies
- Implement standardized processes for technology integration
- Balance technology investment with traditional methods
- Create client education approaches for new visualization methods

Larger Practices (20+ People)

- Consider dedicated visualization specialists within the team
- Develop a technology roadmap aligned with practice development
- Create a structured client introduction to advanced visualization
- Implement formal technology evaluation processes

Technology Implementation by Practice Size

Scaling Technology Investment to Practice Resources

PRACTICE SIZE	TECHNOLOGY APPROACH	FOCUS AREAS	RESOURCES REQUIRED
SMALL PRACTICES (1-5 PEOPLE)	ACCESSIBLE TECHNOLOGIES WITH LOW BARRIERS	• ACTCAD FOR 2D/3D DRAFTING (AUTOCAD ALTERNATIVE) • CLOUD-BASED SOFTWARE SUBSCRIPTIONS • SMARTPHONE/TABLET AR APPLICATIONS • ONLINE RENDERING SERVICES • PARTNERSHIP WITH SPECIALIZED CONSULTANTS	• ₹15,000-50,000 ANNUAL SOFTWARE BUDGET • EXISTING DEVICES (PHONES, TABLETS) • 2-4 HOURS MONTHLY FOR LEARNING • NETWORK OF SPECIALIST PARTNERS
MID-SIZE PRACTICES (6-20 PEOPLE)	DEVELOP INTERNAL EXPERTISE IN STRATEGIC TECHNOLOGIES	• 1-2 CORE VISUALIZATION SOFTWARE PLATFORMS • STANDARDIZED HARDWARE SETUP • TEAM TRAINING PROGRAMS • CLIENT EDUCATION PROCESSES	• ₹1,00,000-3,00,000 ANNUAL TECHNOLOGY BUDGET • DEDICATED WORKSTATIONS (2-3 UNITS) • 1 TEAM MEMBER AS TECHNOLOGY LEAD • MONTHLY TEAM TRAINING SESSIONS
LARGER PRACTICES (20+ PEOPLE)	DEDICATED VISUALIZATION SPECIALISTS AND COMPREHENSIVE SYSTEMS	• FULL VISUALIZATION DEPARTMENT • ADVANCED RENDERING INFRASTRUCTURE • VR/AR PRESENTATION SUITES • TECHNOLOGY ROADMAP PLANNING	• ₹5,00,000+ ANNUAL TECHNOLOGY INVESTMENT • SPECIALIZED STAFF (1-3 VISUALIZATION EXPERTS) • DEDICATED PRESENTATION SPACES • FORMAL TECHNOLOGY EVALUATION PROCESSES

Client Education for Technology Engagement

New visualization technologies often require client education:

1. **Expectation Setting** - What the technology can and cannot show
2. **Interaction Training** - Simple instruction on how to engage with the technology
3. **Interpretation Guidance** - How to understand what they're experiencing
4. **Decision Facilitation** - Structured methods to capture feedback from technology experiences

Successful implementation includes this educational component rather than assuming client familiarity.

Future-Ready Without Future-Obsessed

The visualization technology landscape will continue evolving rapidly. A sustainable approach:

- **Core Competency Maintenance** - Ensure foundational visualization skills remain strong
- **Strategic Experimentation** - Test new technologies in controlled, low-risk applications
- **Client-Led Adoption** - Let client needs drive technology implementation
- **Value-Based Evaluation** - Assess technologies based on outcome improvement, not novelty

This balanced approach keeps your practice current without becoming distracted by every new technology.

Chapter Summary:

Technology With Purpose

The most successful visualization technology implementation focuses not on having the latest tools but on purposefully integrating technology that enhances client understanding and decision-making. Maintaining a client-centered approach to technology adoption ensures that innovation serves project outcomes rather than becoming an end in itself.

Next Client Meeting Action Steps:

1. Evaluate client technology comfort before selecting visualization approaches
2. Choose technologies that address specific communication challenges in the project
3. Prepare appropriate client guidance for any new visualization technologies
4. Balance technology with traditional methods based on client feedback

Chapter 8

Visualization as Business Development

From Project Tool to Practice Builder

Visualization is not just a project delivery component—it's a powerful business development tool when strategically deployed. This chapter examines how to leverage visualization to build your practice, drawing from our experience growing from individual practitioners to an established firm with projects across India.

The Visualization-Centered Marketing Approach

Traditional architecture marketing focuses on completed projects. Visualization-centered marketing shifts this focus to include your thinking process and approach, creating opportunities before projects exist.

The four components of visualization-centered marketing:

1. **Concept Visualization** - Sharing design thinking through speculative projects
2. **Process Transparency** - Revealing your approach through visualization progression
3. **Expertise Demonstration** - Using visualization to showcase specialized knowledge
4. **Value Articulation** - Visual communication of your unique value proposition

Strategic Portfolio Development

Your visualization portfolio should be strategically curated to:

- **Demonstrate Range Within Focus** - Show variety within your specialization
- **Highlight Process and Outcome** - Include development visualization, not just final images
- **Showcase Distinctive Approaches** - Emphasize your unique visualization methods
- **Target Desired Project Types** - Present work aligned with growth objectives

Case Example: When seeking to expand into retail design, we created a series of speculative retail visualizations exploring brand translation to space. These concept visualizations secured our first major retail client despite having no built projects in the sector, demonstrating how strategic visualization can open new markets.

The Cascading Visualization Method

Rather than creating separate marketing materials, implement a cascading approach where project visualizations serve multiple purposes:

- **Project Delivery** - The Primary purpose: serving current clients
- **Case Studies** - Secondary use: showcasing process and outcomes
- **Capability Marketing**: Tertiary use demonstrating expertise
- **Social Content** - Quaternary use engaging broader audiences

This approach maximizes return on visualization investment by creating a continuous business development pipeline from project work.

Visualization for Different Marketing Channels

Effective visualization marketing adapts to different channels:

Website and Portfolio

- Emphasis on comprehensive project storytelling
- Process and outcome presentation
- Detailed contextual information
- High-resolution, detailed visualization

Social Media

- Single impactful images that work at a small scale
- Brief, compelling visual narratives
- Process glimpses that humanize the practice
- Visualization that provokes engagement

Presentations and Talks

- Sequential visualization showing the thinking process
- Comparative examples demonstrating the approach
- Problem-solution visualization pairing
- Before/after transformation emphasis

Publications and Press

- Visualization that communicates core project concepts quickly
- Images that work in both print and digital contexts
- Visualization that tells a clear story without extensive text
- Distinctive approaches that differentiate from typical publication content

Speculative Visualization as Market Entry

Strategically created speculative visualization can open new markets:

1. **Research Target Sector** - Understand specific visualization expectations
2. **Identify Common Challenges** - Focus on problems your approach could solve
3. **Create Problem-Solution Visualizations** - Show your thinking applied to these challenges
4. **Develop Distinctive Viewpoint** - Present a perspective that differentiates your approach

This method has helped us enter new sectors from retail to hospitality without prior built work in those categories.

Client Education Through Visualization

Position yourself as a thought leader through visualization that educates potential clients:

- **Concept Explanation** - Visualizing architectural principles for non-architects
- **Process Illumination** - Showing how design development works
- **Value Demonstration** - Visualizing the impact of design decisions
- **Comparative Analysis** - Illustrating different approaches and their outcomes

This educational content serves as a "no-risk" introduction to your thinking for potential clients.

The Book as Business Development

This very book exemplifies visualization as business development, sharing expertise, and an approach to connect with potential clients. A strategic architecture book:

- **Demonstrates Thinking** - Shows your approach and philosophy
- **Establishes Authority** - Positions you as an expert in your field
- **Creates Recognition** - Builds awareness of your practice
- **Generates Opportunities** - Opens conversations with potential clients

Our experience confirms that sharing knowledge creates more opportunities than it gives away a competitive advantage.

Building a Visualization Content Strategy

Develop a systematic approach to visualization marketing:

1. **Core Content Development** - Create foundation visualization assets
2. **Channel Adaptation** - Modify core content for different platforms
3. **Consistent Cadence** - Maintain regular visualization sharing
4. **Engagement Measurement** - Track which visualizations generate a response
5. **Refinement Loop** - Adjust approach based on audience engagement

This structured approach ensures that visualization marketing becomes a sustainable business development channel rather than an occasional effort.

Visualization Ethics in Marketing

Maintain credibility through ethical visualization practices:

- **Clarity About Status** - Clear distinction between built, in-progress, and conceptual work
- **Attribution Transparency** - Honest credit for collaboration and contributions
- **Realistic Representation** - Avoiding misleading visualization techniques
- **Process Honesty** - Authentic representation of design development

Ethical visualization builds long-term trust that translates to sustainable business growth.

Chapter Summary:

Visualization as Practice Builder

Strategic use of visualization for business development creates opportunities beyond project-by-project growth. By developing a visualization-centered marketing approach, you transform project tools into powerful practice-building assets that communicate your value, demonstrate your thinking, and connect with potential clients before projects even exist.

Next Business Development Steps:

1. Audit your existing visualization assets for marketing potential
2. Develop a visualization sharing calendar across appropriate channels
3. Create speculative visualizations targeting desired market segments
4. Implement a system to track business development results from visualization sharing

CONCLUSION

The Future of Architectural Visualization

As we conclude our exploration of strategic architectural visualization, it's worth considering not just where visualization has been, but where it's headed—and how practitioners can position themselves for continued success in a rapidly evolving landscape.

Beyond Technology to Strategy

The most significant insight throughout this book has been that visualization success depends more on strategic application than technical execution. This principle will become even more critical as visualization technology continues to advance.

As artificial intelligence, real-time rendering, extended reality, and other technologies make high-quality visualization increasingly accessible, the competitive advantage will shift further toward strategic application. Corporate identity through knowing not just how to create compelling images, but when and how to use them for maximum client impact.

The Enduring Human Element

Despite technological advancement, the fundamental purpose of architectural visualization remains unchanged: to help clients see possibilities they cannot envision on their own. This human connection—the bridge between architectural expertise and client aspirations—will remain the core value of visualization regardless of how it's created.

The most successful practitioners will be those who maintain focus on this human element, using technology as an enabler rather than an end in itself. As visualization becomes more immersive and

interactive, the opportunity to create deeper emotional connections with clients will only increase.

Practical Next Steps

As you implement the strategies from this book in your practice, consider these practical next steps:

Immediate Implementation

1. Audit your current visualization approach against the client-centered principles in Chapter 1
2. Identify opportunities to sequence visualization more strategically as outlined in Chapter 2
3. Adapt specialized techniques from Chapters 3-5 to your specific project types
4. Begin developing your distinctive visualization signature following Chapter 6
5. Evaluate technology integration opportunities based on Chapter 7
6. Implement visualization-centered marketing approaches from Chapter 8

Medium-Term Development

1. Create a visualization strategy document for your practice
2. Develop client education materials about your visualization approach
3. Build a visualization portfolio that showcases strategic application, not just technical excellence
4. Implement a feedback system to track which visualization approaches most effectively win projects

Long-Term Evolution

1. Regularly reassess visualization technology investments based on client impact
2. Develop a distinctive visualization philosophy that transcends specific technologies
3. Build recognition for your unique visualization approach
4. Consider the visualization strategy as a core competitive advantage

A Personal Note

When Anjali and I founded our practice in 1991, we could not have imagined how profoundly visualization would transform architectural practice. From hand drawings to digital models to immersive experiences, we've continually adapted our approach while maintaining focus on the fundamental purpose: helping clients see possibilities.

Throughout this evolution, the most valuable lesson has been that visualization is not primarily about showing clients what a design will look like—it's about helping them see what their life or business could become within that design. The most powerful visualizations aren't those that show buildings or spaces, but those that show possibilities and potential.

Whether you're a solo practitioner or part of a large firm, whether you specialize in residential, commercial, or institutional work, whether you create visualizations by hand or with the latest technology—this fundamental principle remains your most powerful competitive advantage.

The future of architectural visualization belongs not to those with the most advanced technology or the most artistic skill, but to those who most effectively use visualization to connect with clients, communicate value, and build confidence. It belongs to those who understand that visualization isn't just about showing design—it's about winning projects.

I hope the strategies in this book help you do exactly that.

About the Author

Mahindra Chawla is an architect and interior designer with over three decades of experience transforming architectural concepts into built realities across Mumbai, Bangalore, Delhi, and beyond.

A graduate of L S Raheja School of Architecture, Mumbai, where he ranked top in Design among all three architecture schools in his first year (1983), Mahindra's journey from academic excellence to professional mastery took an ironic turn—despite his design prowess, he initially struggled with the 'Professional Practice' subject in his final year. This early challenge would prove prophetic, as the subsequent three decades of hands-on practice became his true education in what it means to run a successful architectural business. Today, professional practice—once his greatest academic challenge—has become the very expertise he seeks to share with others. Mahindra began his career learning interior design fundamentals at Space Consultants under Mrs. Kiram Patki.

In 1991, Mahindra and his wife, Anjali, also an interior designer, established their independent practice. From their first project—a poultry feed factory in Tarapore—their work has expanded to include hundreds of high-end residential interiors, corporate offices, and structural repair projects across India.

Notable projects include luxury residences in Mumbai's Bandra and Powai areas, corporate offices across Mumbai's business districts, the structural renovation of BAGD School in Chembur, and projects extending to Bangalore, Lonavala, Aamby Valley, Delhi, Pune, and Vapi.

A career highlight came in 2012 when they won a private competition for the interior design and turnkey contracting of The Consulate General of Malaysia's office in BKC, Mumbai—their first design-build project. The exemplary execution, completed 15 days ahead of schedule, earned high appreciation from the Consul General (Trade)

Mr. Hadi, establishing the firm's reputation for delivering complex projects with precision and efficiency.

The practice's strength in providing comprehensive interior design and build services under a single window has cultivated lasting client relationships. Distinguished clients including the former City Engineer of Thane (four projects over two decades), the former Vice President of CRISIL, Managing Directors of Kimatram & Sons, The Lotus Group (real estate developers), and Spacecom Group of Companies—along with other prominent real estate developers—consistently return to Chawla N Associates for their evolving space requirements, testament to the firm's reliability and design excellence.

Professional recognition has accompanied this client's success. During their early decade of practice, several projects were featured in The Times of India's address section, bringing public attention to their innovative work. More recently, the Eldrok India Architecture Awards 2022 honoured Chawla N Associates for Excellence in Interior Turnkey Contracting Service at the Eldrok India Architectural Summit on June 2nd, 2022, recognizing three decades of consistent professional achievement.

Mahindra Chawla and Anjali Chawla are the founders of **Chawla N Associates**, a practice known for its integrated approach to interior design and architecture. His core expertise lies in 'interior design and build' projects, with additional specialization in structural repair work. Beyond practice, Mahindra is developing "Design Practice Mastery," an online coaching program for practicing interior designers. Having learned through decades of hands-on experience what isn't taught in architecture schools, he now shares the practical insights and methodologies that have made his practice successful over three decades.
Visualization Advantage is Mahindra's first book. It distills decades of client interaction and project visualization into practical strategies for architectural professionals worldwide.

For speaking engagements, consulting, or project inquiries, Mahindra can be reached through Chawla N Associates.

Website: https://ChawlaNassociates.com

https://ChawlaNassociates.com

Email: VisualizationAdvantage@Gmail.com

VisualAdvantage@Gmail.com

LinkedIn Connect: Chawla N Associates
LinkedIn: www.LinkedIn.com/in/ChawlaNassociates

LinkedIn Connect

We Value Your Feedback

Thank you for reading **Visualization Advantage**! Your insights and experiences help us create better resources for the architectural and interior design community and improve future editions of this book.

Share Your Thoughts

Please take a few minutes to share your feedback and let us know how these visualization strategies are working in your practice:

Reader Feedback Form: https://forms.gle/hxTRFksnxY7MC9J4A

Reader's Feedback Form

Your Feedback Helps Us:

- **Improve future editions** of this book based on real-world applications
- **Understand the biggest visualization challenges** architects & interior designers are facing today
- **Develop new resources** that address your specific needs
- **Connect with fellow practitioners** who are implementing these strategies
- **Celebrate success stories** when these techniques help you win projects

Success Stories Welcome

We'd love to hear when these visualization techniques help you win a project! Email us your success stories - they inspire us and help other architects see the practical value of strategic visualization.

Thank you for being part of our mission to help architects communicate more effectively and win more valuable projects.

- Mahindra Chawla